Contents

ENGINEERED FOR SUCCESS:

A HANDBOOK OF
CHRISTIAN ENGINEERING

Engineered *Truth* That, When
Applied to Your *Spirit, Will* Result
in Spiritual *Growth* and *Success*

John A Peters

WESTBOW
PRESS
A DIVISION OF THOMAS NELSON

WestBow Press books may be ordered through booksellers or by contacting:

WestBow Press
A Division of Thomas Nelson
1663 Liberty Drive
Bloomington, IN 47403
www.westbowpress.com
1-(866) 928-1240

ISBN: 978-1-4497-6809-6 (sc)
ISBN: 978-1-4497-6808-9 (e)
ISBN: 978-1-4497-6810-2 (hc)

Library of Congress Control Number: 2012917595

Printed in the United States of America

WestBow Press rev. date:09/27/2012

This book is dedicated to my parents Henry Alexander Peters and Denise Elizabeth Peters, who first taught me how to write. To my wife Elistra, who taught me how to succeed, and to my two children Josh and Jevonne, who taught me how to persevere.

Preface

This design manual is designed to build and re-engineer lives. Jehovah, the Great Engineer built the world from nothing and then built man in his own image and likeness. God then released the male-man and female-man with an assignment to continue building on the earth. Every believer has been released with a mandate from God to be an engineer on the earth. *Engineered for Success* is a reference source for believers with an interest in re-engineering their spirits. It introduces the concept of *engineered truth* and defines it as the design and construction of truth. The author is a civil engineer by profession and has worked in several Caribbean countries.

This handbook contains inspirational messages that will build your spirit and place you on the growth path of life.

The author hopes that all interested in building lives will be blessed by the truth released in this work.

Introduction

The word *success* is only found once in the Bible—Joshua 1:8. In that verse, God tells Joshua to meditate on his truth day and night in order to prosper and have success. The Holy Spirit has been given the mandate to lead us into all truth, and he designs and constructs truth in our lives. This is *engineered truth.* It is God's truth that will engineer you for success. God's purpose is for you to be engineered for success by His truth. The principles of engineering, therefore, can point the way to God's truth. The following sections introduce the various principles of engineering and then point to the truths contained in God's Word. Be blessed, and be successful.

Section 1

Design Analysis

Therefore whoever hears these sayings of Mine, and does them, I will liken him to a wise man who built his house on the rock: and the rains descended, the floods came, and the winds blew and beat on that house: and it did not fall, for it was founded on rock.

But everyone who hears these sayings of Mine, and does not do them, will be like the foolish man who built his house on the sand: and the rain descended, the floods came, and the winds blew and beat on that house; and it fell. And great was its fall.

—Matthew 7:26–27

When designing a building, the structural engineer will first start with the roof, and based on the loadings, the engineer will perform the design from the top down to the foundation. This means that the foundation is the last component designed in a building. The design engineer must know the height of the building and what loads are imposed on the building.

The Engineer will design for the maximum wind loads and the earthquake forces that may occur where the building is located. The Engineer must know what will be the final use of the building to estimate the live loads, whether it is an office or cinema or church. The live loads are the occupancy loads, such as the furniture or the people that will occupy the building and those loads can change in location. The roof beams must support the roof slab, which has to be supported by the columns below. The same goes for the next floor until one reaches the ground floor. The ground floor columns must support all the loads above, and the foundation must support these column loads.

In the same way, when God built you, he determined the loads you would carry and the maximum wind loads you would incur from the storms that would blow in your direction. God knew how much shaking you would face from the situations and circumstances in your life.

He knew the live loads or occupancy loads that you have to carry as part of your life on earth.

So, if we believe that God is an all-powerful God, then we must believe that He truly created us as well-designed beings. God is a wise builder who designed you to withstand the rain, the floods, the winds, and all those who desire to walk on you.

This week, whatever situation may be facing you, know that you have been built to withstand that storm and every shaking under your foot.

So let your faith arise and believe that this God you serve is a wise builder. The rains will come, the floods will rise, the winds will blow, but through it all, this well-designed creature of God will not fall. *Hallelujah!*

Prayer

Father, wisdom belongs to you. I believe you are a wise builder. I trust your Word that I am a well-designed creature. I have been designed to withstand the floods, the winds, and every shaking under my feet. So these storms shall come and go, but I will stand in your presence, on a solid rock. Amen.

Notes

Notes

Section 2

Sound and Vibration

Joshua said to the people: Shout, for the Lord has given you the city! So the people shouted when the priests blew the trumpets. And it happened when the people heard the sound of the trumpet that the wall fell down flat.

—Joshua 6:16, 20

One famous engineering disaster was the failure of the Tacoma Narrows Bridge. This bridge, when built, was described by engineers as a feat of engineering. One day, forty-five mile per hour winds caused the bridge to vibrate and sway from side to side. The bridge collapsed into the water below. The engineers described the failure to be caused by "aeroelastic flutter." This was our modern-day Jericho.

Joshua had to face a fortified city as his first battle to possess the Promised Land. It was won with a shout.

There is a time when you will have to shout to break down the walls that stand before the promises of God. The story of Jericho is important in the life of every believer because we need to know each of us will have a Jericho experience.

Jericho was on the border of the Promised Land; to dominate the Promised Land, you had to overthrow Jericho. It controlled the trade routes into Canaan.

For every believer there is a place you must cross, a situation you have to overcome in order to control the trade routes of your promises.

There is an ordained time to shout. "Shout! For the Lord has given you the city."

The walls must come down. Your feet will touch the promises of God.

When God destroys the walls, no man can rebuild them.

This week, ask yourself if you are still marching around your Jericho. If you see that the walls are still standing, then it means that you have not shouted.

The Hebrew word for shout used in this verse is *ruwa*. It means "to split the ear with a sound."

Your Jericho is the place of unfulfilled promises; it is the place where obstacles and walls have been put up to stop you from entering into the fullness of God. You have to release a ruwa-shout to split the ears of the enemy and break down those walls.

And Jesus cried out again with a loud voice, and yielded up His spirit. Then, behold, the veil of the temple was torn in two from top to bottom;

and the earth quaked, and the rocks were split, and the graves were opened; and many bodies of the saints who had fallen asleep were raised; and coming out of the graves after His resurrection, they went into the holy city and appeared to many. (Matthew 27:50–53)

Jesus shouted with a ruwa-voice, "It is finished."

The ruwa-shout rocked heaven and earth; both the natural and spiritual realms shook. The ruwa-shout:

- ripped the veil of the temple,
- ripped apart the rocks, and
- ripped apart the open graves.

You have to release that ruwa-shout to split open your path to the promises of God.

Shout to the Lord with a voice of triumph! Psalm 47; 1

John A. Peters

Prayer

Father, there is a Jericho where the trade routes to my destiny are located. There is a ruwa-shout that the heavens and earth must hear. You have given me the city, and I shout that you are Jehovah—El Elyon—the Most High God. I shout to you, God, with the voice of triumph. Every wall shall fall, and I shall walk into the promises of God. Amen.

Notes

Notes

Section 3

Formwork Design

For the earnest expectation of the creation eagerly
waits for the revealing of the sons of God.

—*Romans 8:19*

In reinforced concrete construction, builders use formwork to contain the concrete. This formwork can be constructed from wood, metal, or plastic. Concrete has to be cured, and thus the formwork cannot be immediately removed until the concrete has gained sufficient strength. So until it has been cured sufficiently, the formwork hides its beauty.

The word translated for *reveal* has a root word in Greek that means "to take the cover off." God always hides away something until it is fully formed.

A child is only released from the mother's womb when it is fully formed and can face the new environment outside.

Jesus began his ministry when he was deemed fully mature and formed. The formwork was removed, and he was revealed to the world.

The book of Exodus speaks of Moses hiding away in Midian until God desired for him to be revealed to Pharaoh; the formwork was removed, and he went to his father in law and said to him, " Please let me go and return to my brethren who are in Egypt – Exodus 4:18. If the formwork is removed too early, the entire structure will collapse. For many of us, the time hiding beneath the formwork is difficult. When you are in the formwork, the world cannot see you. Despite all your abilities and talents, you have to stay confined.

We must allow God to fully form us when we are hiding inside the formwork. Many push away the formwork and get into all sorts of problems. The concrete has to wait until it is fully cured and strong enough before the formwork can be removed, and then the showcasing of all its beauty can begin.

This week, as you ponder these words, know that God has placed you in formwork to fully set you as a son of the Most High God.

Wait on the Lord to fully cure you and set you, and he will release you in due season.

Prayer

Father, you have placed me inside the formwork so that I can be fully formed and set to fulfill my destiny upon the Earth. Teach me not to push against the formwork but to wait in that hidden place until you decide to release me and reveal me. I shall wait on the Lord until he takes the cover off. Amen.

Notes

Notes

Section 4

Scaffolding Design

Then he dreamed, and behold, a ladder was set up on the earth, and its top reached to heaven: and there the angels of God were ascending and descending on it. And behold, the Lord stood above it and said: "I am the Lord God of Abraham your father and the God of Isaac: the land on which you lie I will give you and your descendants.

—Genesis 28:12–13

Scaffolding has been used in the construction of tall structures in many ancient cultures. History has recorded its use by the Egyptians, Nubians, Chinese, and Greeks. You will see it on every construction site today.

Jacob saw the largest scaffolding ever in his dream. Here was a scaffolding joining heaven to earth and which had angels ascending and descending.

Before Jacob reached this place, his life was indeed tumultuous. His story up to this point was one of lies, deceit, and destruction. His mother had encouraged him in a deceitful plot in an attempt to bring to pass a prophetic word. When we cannot wait for God to fulfill his plans in our lives, we attempt to force his plans into existence with the destruction that results from our actions.

How many people get into wrong relationships and marriages because they could not wait on God?

When you look at the story of Jacob in the book of Genesis, we see that God had spoken to Rebekah in Genesis 25:22–23 before the boys were born.

> *But the children struggled within her: and she said, "If all is well, why am I like this?" So she went to inquire of the Lord. And the Lord said to her: "Two nations are in your womb, two people shall be separated from your body: One people shall be stronger than the other, And the older shall serve the younger." (Genesis 25:22–23)*

God revealed his plans for the two boys to Rebekah before they were born. God wanted two nations to arise from Jacob's sons, with the younger serving the older. Both boys were blessed to be nation-builders, yet the younger would be stronger. God would have established his plan in his own time.

It would appear that Rebekah never told Isaac about what the Lord had revealed to her concerning the two boys. So when Isaac loved Esau more, she planned the deceit to ensure that God's plans would be established.

Later on in Genesis, we read that she hatches a plan to deceive Isaac. Jacob to his credit advises his mother that such deceit will bring a curse and not a blessing.

The results of Rebekah's botched plan were:

a.   Esau now hates his brother and plans to kill him.

b.   Isaac can no longer trust his wife.

c.   Jacob has to run away.

Rebekah's lack of faith in believing God at his word and waiting for God's promise caused much destruction.

Wait for the promise!

Learn this week to wait on the promises of God and do not try and help God accomplish his plans.

Prayer

> *Father, I will wait on you. Teach me today to know your timing is impeccable, that there is no too late or too early. You will always be a right-on-time God. Amen.*

Notes

Notes

Section 5

Highway Design

A highway shall be there, and a road and it shall be called the Highway of Holiness. The unclean shall not pass over it, but it shall be for others. Whoever walks the road, although a fool shall not go astray. No lion shall be there, nor any ravenous beast go up on it; it shall not be found there. But the redeemed shall walk there,.

—*Isaiah 35:8–9*

We often associate the word *highway* with our modern understanding of the term. The word highway today conjures images of a wide multilane roadway. So when we read "Highway of Holiness," we think of a wide, straight road. The word highway that is used here in the book of Isaiah

35:8 is the only time the Hebrew word *macluwl* is used in the Bible. The word means "an elevated road."

The word highway was in fact used to describe Roman roads, which were built as *high* ways. The roads were elevated to ensure that when the Roman armies were going through plains, they would be able to see an enemy hiding in the bushes.

With this understanding of the word, we have a different perspective on the Scripture in Isaiah 35:8. There is a high, elevated road of holiness, and those who travel that elevated road will always see the enemy lurking in the dark.

Isaiah said that those who walk on that road shall not go astray. Indeed, like the Roman soldiers, if you travel this high way or elevated road, you will be able to see the schemes and traps of the enemy. So many believers fall into traps because they have not walked that elevated road of holiness.

On this high way, the ravenous beast cannot climb to reach the surface. There is protection for God's people on this Highway of Holiness.

Believers have faith to believe God will heal their bodies. We ask God to heal us from sickness and disease, yet the other part of us, our spirit, is never the subject of requests to God. When was the last time you asked God to fill you with his holiness? We are constantly dissecting ourselves, yet God sees us as a spirit with a soul and a body.

The same vigor with which we ask God for things relating to our body— may they be healing or the provision of a house or car—we should also use to ask for the things for our spirit. Tell God that you want to be holy as he is holy. Tell him you want to walk the Highway of Holiness that he has prepared for his saints.

We need to be on this Highway of Holiness at these times in our lives, as there are indeed ravenous beasts around. On this road, you receive wisdom and understanding, discernment and insight, protection and comfort.

Tell your Father God this week that your desire is to walk and stay on this Highway of Holiness.

Prayer

Father, my desire is to walk and stay on your Highway of Holiness. Let me walk in that place where no ravenous beast can enter. Release your wisdom and understanding, discernment and insight, protection and comfort. I ask this in no other name but the name of your son, Jesus Christ. Amen."

Notes

Notes

Section 6

Soil Mechanics

But why do you call Me 'Lord, Lord,' and not do the things which I say? Whoever comes to Me, and hears My sayings and does them, I will show you whom he is like: He is like a man building a house, who dug deep and laid the foundation on the rock. And when the flood arose, the stream beat vehemently against that house, and could not shake it, for it was founded on the rock. But he who heard and did nothing is like a man who built a house on the earth without a foundation, against which the stream beat vehemently; and immediately it fell. And the ruin of that house was great.

—Luke 6:46–49

In soil mechanics and foundation engineering, the engineering properties of the geological materials named *soil* and *rock* are studied. Based on these properties, the foundations of structures are designed by engineers. When poor soils are encountered, either we "dig down" .'til we reach the better soils or rock and place the foundation on this material, or we pile through the poor soils. Piled foundation can involve the driving of piles to bedrock, and the building is therefore designed based on the support from the rock.

Genesis 38 is an account of the life of Judah, one of the sons of Joseph's brothers, that is oddly placed between Chapter 37 and Chapter 39. When you read Genesis Chapter 37, it speaks of the life of Joseph and Chapter 39 continues from where Chapter 37 ends.

So why is Chapter 38 so important to us? Why should the story of Joseph be interrupted to convey a spiritual concept as seen in Genesis Chapter 38?

God is not a God of chance, but a God of purpose, so there is a divine purpose for this interruption.

The first half of Chapter 38 sets the scene for the last half which occurs over a shorter time period.

> *Now it came to pass, at the time for giving birth, that behold, twins were in her womb. And so it was, when she was giving birth, that the one put out his hand; and the midwife took a scarlet thread and bound it on his hand, saying, "This one came out first." Then it happened, as he drew back his hand, that his brother came out unexpectedly; and she said, "How did you break through? This breach be upon you!" Therefore his name was called Perez. Afterward his brother came out who had the scarlet thread on his hand. And his name was called Zerah. (Genesis 38: 27–30)*

One of the twins appears by his hand, and a scarlet thread was placed on his hand to signify he was first. Miraculously, he draws back his hand

and his brother comes out first. He was called *Perez*—"breakthrough." Then the other twin with the scarlet thread comes out, and he is called *Zerah*—"rising in glory."

God was laying a spiritual principle here that *perez* will always be before *zerah*.

You have to break through to rise in glory!

So when the story of Joseph resumes in Genesis Chapter 39, he is on his way to be a slave in Egypt in the house of Potiphar.

Joseph has to break through the fear, the shame, and the dishonor of being a slave in order to rise in glory.

Joseph had to *perez* to move to *zerah*.

In Genesis 39:20, Joseph ends up in prison, indeed a maximum security prison, where the king's prisoners are held. Yet again he has to *perez* to *zerah*.

He broke through death, deceit, lies and rose again.

> Then Pharaoh said to Joseph, "Inasmuch as God has shown you all this, there is no one as discerning and wise as you. You shall be over my house, and all my people shall be ruled according to your word; only in regard to the throne will I be greater than you." And Pharaoh said to Joseph, "See, I have set you over all the land of Egypt."
>
> Then Pharaoh took his signet ring off his hand and put it on Joseph's hand; and he clothed him in garments of fine linen and put a gold chain around his neck. And he had him ride in the second chariot which he had; and they cried out before him, "Bow the knee!" So he set him over all the land of Egypt. Pharaoh also said to Joseph, "I am Pharaoh, and without your consent no man may lift his hand or foot in all the land of Egypt." And Pharaoh

> *called Joseph's name Zaphnath-Paaneah. And he gave him as*
> *a wife Asenath, the daughter of Poti-Pherah priest of On. So*
> *Joseph went out over all the land of Egypt. (Genesis 41:39–45)*

Joseph rose in glory and honor because he broke through disappointment, deceit, lies, and hurts.

Until you can break through, you will not rise in glory.

Every *zerah* experience follows a *perez* experience.

> *Not that I have already attained, or am already perfected; but I press*
> *on, that I may lay hold of that for which Christ Jesus has also laid*
> *hold of me. Brethren, I do not count myself to have apprehended;*
> *but one thing I do, forgetting those things which are behind and*
> *reaching forward to those things which are ahead, I press toward*
> *the goal for the prize of the upward call of God in Christ Jesus.*

Therefore let us, as many as are mature, have this mind; and if in anything you think otherwise, God will reveal even this to you. Nevertheless, to the degree that we have already attained, let us walk by the same rule, let us be of the same mind. (Philippians 3:12–15)

The words *lay hold* mean "to seize suddenly as in a surprise attack." It is like pushing hard against a door of a building until it collapses, and then running in and seize whatever is inside.

Many believers stand at the door waiting for it to open. This mindset has been formed by the theology we have been fed. So we are told to plant a seed and expect a miracle in return. Yet God places the opportunities behind the door, and we have no urgency to push it down to get what God has reserved for us.

The obstacles will be there, but you have to push through to get the promises, there will always be a *perez* experience before a *zerah* experience. Whether in you school or at your business, this spiritual principle stands.

"But why do you call Me 'Lord, Lord,' and not do the things which I say? Whoever comes to Me, and hears My sayings and does them, I will show you whom he is like: He is like a man building a house, who dug deep and laid the foundation on the rock. And when the flood arose, the stream beat vehemently against that house, and could not shake it, for it was founded on the rock. 49 But he who heard and did nothing is like a man who built a house on the earth without a foundation, against which the stream beat vehemently; and immediately it fell. And the ruin of that house was great." (Luke 6:46–49)

The geology of the surrounding area was such that there was a layer of soil from the deposits of the river when it overflowed its banks over the years. The rock was below. Those who pressed through and dug through the soil and broke through the rock were rewarded with a house that could not shake.

We have to learn to continue digging until we reach rock.

There is only one way to rise in glory; there has to be *perez* before *zerah*.

Prayer

Father, today I purpose in my heart to dig until I reach rock, and despite the many obstacles that I face, I will not give up. I will push through the disappointment and I will push through the setbacks, for I know that there is zerah experience for me. I shall rise in glory. Indeed I and the children that Jehovah has given me are for signs and wonders on this earth. I declare this today in Jesus' name. Amen.

Notes

Notes

Section 7

Water Resource Management

For My people have committed two evils:

They have forsaken Me, the fountain of living waters,

And hewn themselves cisterns—broken
cisterns that can hold no water.

—Jeremiah 2:13

Clean water is an essential component of people's health. The economy of a country can be determined by its water supply. Countries that are managing their water resource must now proceed with a more holistic and integrated approach which considers the whole water cycle.

All countries need to implement an integrated water resource management (IWRM) policy which must focus on understanding all of the water resources available to its communities. Policy makers must actively pursue and care for those resources and provide solutions that best match an area's water needs and constraints.

So water plays a significant role in our physical lives, and Jeremiah was speaking of the failure of a people to effectively manage their spiritual water resources.

In order to fully understand the significance of this Scripture and the powerful truth that lies within it, you have to know how springs are formed.

A springs flows because the pressure in the aquifer (water-bearing soil or rock) which is covered by a confining layer (e.g. clay) is greater than the atmospheric pressure at the land. A spring is formed when the water reaches the surface through a fracture or porous layer.

The water is normally cool, clear, and flowing under pressure, gushing out for everyone to enjoy. All you have to do is to position yourself in the location of the spring and drink and be refreshed. It flows in the dry season and in the rainy season.

A cistern is formed by excavation into the rock, involving considerable effort. In biblical times, this chiseling was time-consuming and the very hard work was done only with hand tools. When the cistern is dug, you then have to bring water to fill it up, and seepage will happen because of small cracks in the rock. How sad it is that many of us prefer to dig broken cisterns, instead of going to the fountain of living water and being refreshed?

> *"He who believes in Me, as the Scripture has said, out*
> *of his heart will flow rivers of living water." But this He*
> *spoke concerning the Spirit, whom those believing in*
> *Him would receive; for the Holy Spirit was not yet given,*
> *because Jesus was not yet glorified. (John 7:38–39)*

God has sent his Holy Spirit as the fountain of living water. This living water is for us to drink, to be refreshed by, yet we have instead gone about digging rocks and hauling water, and the water is seeping away. We are in this continual cycle and never experiencing the joy of the Lord. Let us all stop digging broken cisterns and begin to drink from the fountain of life.

> *None of the fruits of the Spirit can be obtained by digging*
> *cisterns. The love, the joy, peace, patience, kindness, goodness,*
> *faithfulness, gentleness, and self-control will leak out if*
> *we go about digging cisterns. (Galatians 5:22–23)*

If we live in the Spirit let us also walk in the Spirit. (Galatians 5:25)

The word *walk* describes a present tense activity; it is a "now" word. There is a response that heaven is waiting for you to engage. We need to drink from the fountain today and be refreshed; don't dig cisterns that will leak.

Prayer

Father, today I repent of digging cisterns and placing water that leaks away. I desire to drink from your fountain and to see the joy, love, peace, patience, kindness, goodness, and gentleness continually flow in my life. Amen.

Notes

Notes

Section 8

Military Engineering Part 1

*Fight the good fight of faith, lay hold on eternal life,
to which you were also called and have confessed the
good confession in the presence of many witnesses.*

—*1 Timothy 6:12*

Military engineering is defined as the art and the practice of designing, building, and maintaining military work and lines of military transport and communications. It involves tactical support on the battlefield, construction of fortifications, demolition of enemy installations, and strategic support. The strategic support involves construction or maintenance of airfields, ports, roads, railroads, bridges, and hospitals. The Great Wall of China represents one of the works of military engineers. The Romans also maintained their power and rule through their strong military engineering expertise.

Believers must also maintain their strength through strong military engineering. So it is important to know your weapons of war.

> *Put on the whole armor of God, that you may be able to*
> *stand against the wiles of the devil. For we do not wrestle*
> *against flesh and blood, but against principalities, against*
> *powers, against the rulers of the darkness of this age, against*
> *spiritual hosts of wickedness in the heavenly places. Therefore*
> *take up the whole armor of God, that you may be able to*
> *withstand in the evil day, and having done all, to stand.*
>
> *Stand therefore, having girded your waist with truth, having put*
> *on the breastplate of righteousness, and having shod your feet with*
> *the preparation of the gospel of peace; above all, taking the shield*
> *of faith with which you will be able to quench all the fiery darts of*
> *the wicked one. And take the helmet of salvation, and the sword*
> *of the Spirit, which is the word of God...(Ephesians 6:11–17).*

The illustrations used by the apostle Paul were used purely to convey the weaponry available at the time. Paul was describing the Roman soldier because Rome had the finest military machine at that time. The Romans were the "super power."

The creativity of man is a God-given characteristic. Therefore, if we look at the weapons of modern warfare we will get an insight into the spiritual weapons and the extent of the battle.

We need to upgrade our language and begin to speak about launching missiles into the second heaven, engaging submarines and aircraft carriers to deal with marine spirits.

Unfortunately, we are locked into a thought process of two thousand years ago, about swords and helmets and shields.

When was the last time you launched a *smart bomb* against the Enemy? Upgrade your prayer language to modern warfare!

If we look at the technology of present day war, you would see three types of weapons:

- Weapons for the air
- Weapons for the ground
- Weapons for the sea

Our battle with the enemy is a battle in the air (heavenlies), a battle for the ground and a battle for the sea. *God* has given us weapons for the various battles we have to face. *Upgrade your thinking!*

Modern Weaponry

Rocket-propelled grenades: destroys tanks, helicopters, and buildings

Nuclear bombs: destroys whole cities, nations, and kingdoms

Bunker busters: destroys underground targets

Cruise missiles: can deliver a one thousand pound bomb over one thousand miles away

Smart bomb: most accurate weaponry

Sidewinder missiles: can find a target on their own without need of human guidance

Patriot missiles: designed to detect, target, and then destroy incoming missiles

Every situation demands a different weapon.

If for example, you are sick and you do know what is causing the sickness, then a *sidewinder missile prayer* when released will find its target on its own.

When your son is in trouble and you are miles away from him, then you release a cruise missile prayer and a *one thousand pound prayer bomb* is released to go up to one thousand miles away and destroy its target.

When the enemy launches missiles toward you and blocks the release of your blessing, you need a *patriot missile* to detect, target, and destroy every incoming missile and punch a hole into the second heaven to bring that blessing from heaven to earth.

There are times the enemy will come after your property, and you need to know how to use your ground artillery.

Ground Artillery

Machine guns: can release hundreds of bullets in a second

Land mines: when the enemy steps on these, he is blown up

Some of us need to plant some spiritual land mines on our property.

Battle for the Air

Your airspace determines your destiny. If the area above you is controlled by the enemy, the blessings required to release you into your destiny will not come.

F-22 Raptor: One of the most modern military aircraft. Uses stealth technology and carries an array of weapons.

The enemy cannot detect you when you launch a surprise and stealth attack with your *Raptor* weaponry. This is when the gates of hell cannot prevail.

Stealth bombers: These travel long distances undetected by radar and are able to drop nuclear bombs to take out key targets

Upgrade your weaponry!

Battle for the Sea

This is a very important weapon. We need to better understand marine spirits. Water takes up seventy percent of the earth's surface. So a powerful kingdom of marine spirits controls the earth.

Those involved in the deliverance ministry have said that these marine spirits are assigned to destroy marriages. Our lack of knowledge of these marine spirits is evident given the ruthless and relentless attack on marriages.

We need to use our submarines and our sea-fighting weaponry to battle these marine spirits. These marine spirits are deadly and powerful. God spoke to Job about them:

> When he raises himself up, the mighty are afraid;
>
> Because of his crashings they are beside[a] themselves.
>
> *Though* the sword reaches him, it cannot avail;
>
> Nor does spear, dart, or javelin.
>
> He regards iron as straw,
>
> *And* bronze as rotten wood.
>
> The arrow cannot make him flee;
>
> Slingstones become like stubble to him.
>
> Darts are regarded as straw;

He laughs at the threat of javelins. (Job 41:25–29)

You cannot defeat a submarine spirit with sticks and darts and javelins. You need a nuclear warhead missile.

Upgrade your weaponry!

Prayer

"Father, the marine spirits that are attacking my life have caused destruction. Today Lord, I repent for not using the full weaponry of war at my disposal. Even now I release the nuclear warhead missiles to destroy every marine spirit sent to destroy me. Let these missiles detect, target, and destroy the work of these marine spirits. Amen."

Notes

Notes

Section 9

Military Engineering Part 2

In Section 8, we looked at the weapons of our warfare. We saw that God has given us a vast array of weaponry to battle the enemy. We have more than a sword at our disposal. We have missile that can detect, target, and destroy the enemy. Submarines and aircraft carriers to deal with the marine spirits. F-22 Raptor jets to clear the airspace above us to allow God's blessings to flow freely.

But sometimes when we face a stubborn enemy, we need to know the strategies to deal with him.

> But the children of Benjamin did not drive out the Jebusites
> who inhabited Jerusalem; so the Jebusites dwell with the
> children of Benjamin in Jerusalem to this day. (Judges 1:21)

The tribe of Benjamin could not drive out the Jebusites who inhabited Jerusalem. We see also in Joshua 15:63 that the Jebusites had established a stronghold over Jerusalem. Also, they could not be dislodged from the tribe of Judah.

> *As for the Jebusites, the inhabitants of Jerusalem, the children*
> *of Judah could not drive them out; but the Jebusites dwell with*
> *the children of Judah at Jerusalem to this day. (Joshua 15:63)*

The Jebusites had established a stronghold over Jerusalem, such that they could not be dislodged.

God in his mercy chose another Benjamite to drive out the Jebusites. In this case God chose Saul to drive out the Jebusites but he failed. God chose another man from the tribe of Judah, David, to drive out the Jebusites.

At this point the Jebusites considered themselves so strong and entrenched that they said to David that they will send their blind and lame to fight against him.

> *And the king and his men went to Jerusalem against the Jebusites,*
> *the inhabitants of the land, who spoke to David, saying, "You*
> *shall not come in here; but the blind and the lame will repel*
> *you," thinking, "David cannot come in here." Nevertheless David*
> *took the stronghold of Zion (that is, the City of David).*
>
> *Now David said on that day, "Whoever climbs up by way of the*
> *water shaft and defeats the Jebusites (the lame and the blind, who*
> *are hated by David's soul), he shall be chief and captain." Therefore*
> *they say, "The blind and the lame shall not come into the house."*
>
> *Then David dwelt in the stronghold, and called it the City*
> *of David. And David built all around from the Millo and*
> *inward. So David went on and became great, and the*
> *Lord God of hosts was with him. (2 Samuel 6–10)*

Nevertheless, David took the stronghold of Zion.

There is a stronghold in Jerusalem, the Place of Peace, because the devil wants to steal your peace. He does not want you to take possession of Jerusalem.

For each of the enemy's strategies, there is a different weapon of war. For this war against the Jebusite, David's strategy was to go at their most fortified area. The Jebusites had fortified the water shafts, as they believed that this was the most vulnerable area within the city. Some theologians are of the opinion that recent archaeological findings do suggest that these water shafts were the most fortified part of the city.

David went to the most fortified part and attacked. This is the same strategy that Joshua used when he defeated the King of Jerusalem.

> *Then Joshua said, "Open the mouth of the cave, and bring out those five kings to me from the cave." And they did so, and brought out those five kings to him from the cave: the king of Jerusalem, the king of Hebron, the king of Jarmuth, the king of Lachish, and the king of Eglon.*
>
> *So it was, when they brought out those kings to Joshua, that Joshua called for all the men of Israel, and said to the captains of the men of war who went with him, "Come near, put your feet on the necks of these kings." And they drew near and put their feet on their necks. Then Joshua said to them, "Do not be afraid, nor be dismayed; be strong and of good courage, for thus the Lord will do to all your enemies against whom you fight." And afterward Joshua struck them and killed them, and hanged them on five trees; and they were hanging on the trees until evening. (Joshua 10)*

It is time to put your foot on the neck of the enemy who has set up himself as a stronghold. You have to fight the Jebusites this way.

Prayer

Father, you have given us mighty weapons of warfare to go against the strongholds in our lives. Teach me how to use each weapon for each strategy of the enemy. Like Joshua, let my feet be on the neck of the king of the Jebusites, and let these strongholds be destroyed today in Jesus' name. Amen.

Notes

Notes

Section 10

Construction Management

Construction management or construction project management (CPM) is the overall planning, coordination, and control of a project from inception to completion aimed at meeting a client's requirements in order to produce a functionally and financially viable project. CPM is project management that applies to the construction sector.

The Word of God speaks of a construction management project which we should all be aware of.

> "And I tell you that you are Peter, and on this rock I will build my church, and the gates of Hades will not overcome it. I will give you the keys of the kingdom of heaven; whatever you bind

on earth will be bound in heaven, and whatever you loose
on earth will be loosed in heaven." (Matthew 16:18–19

We want to look at verse 18 closer. If we deconstruct this verse, we begin to see some truths Jesus was conveying.

Question 1: Who was the builder?

Answer: Jesus said he will build.

Question 2: Whose church is it?

Answer: Jesus said, "My church," so he is in
possession of this church.

Question 3: What is the church being built to do?

Answer: Jesus said, to prevail against the gates of hell.

Let us put it back together.

There is a building project and Jesus has to function as construction project manager. He calls the functional and viable project he has to produce "the Church." It is to function as being victorious over the powers of the enemy.

So our misconception of "the church" begins to change. The definition of "the Church" therefore has to include the following facts:

1. It is built by Jesus.
2. It belongs to Jesus. It is his project.
3. It has power over the forces of darkness.

So when leaders claim that they have built "the church," it could not be what Jesus was referring to. Also, when one says this is "my church," it is also not what Jesus was talking about. Lastly, when you do not see victory over the powers of darkness, you also cannot call it "the Church."

It is interesting to look at the Greek word for church. The word used is *ekklesia*, a compound of two words.

Ek, meaning "the origin or point where motion or action proceeds," and *kaleo*, meaning "to call aloud or declare."

So if we put the word back together, the Church is an origin or a point from which loud declarations proceed.

It is the intent of God that we become "the Church"—an origin or a point from which loud declarations proceed.

Jesus is building us to become origin points of loud declarations to defeat the powers of darkness.

We therefore need to understand what Jesus is building and working out in our lives.

We must, however, look at Matthew 16:19. The Amplified Bible has a wonderful translation:

I will give you the keys of the kingdom of heaven; and whatever you bind (declare to be improper and unlawful) on earth [e]must be what is already bound in heaven; and whatever you loose (declare lawful) on earth must be what is already loosed in heaven.

These origin points will make loud declarations of what is improper and unlawful on the earth and also declare what is lawful.

The Church is therefore Jesus' elected parliament to pass his agenda on the earth.

So when "the Church" gathers, the parliamentary session is more than singing psalms, hearing a word, and picking up an offering. The parliament meets to declare what is improper on the earth.

If the enemy wants to destroy your child, you have the authority to declare this plan of the enemy is improper on the earth.

You hear saints at times speak as if they are hiding from the enemy, as if so many bullets are being flung in their directions that they are running for cover and hiding in fear.

I once shared with some eleven-year-olds who were about to sit an exam that the enemy comes to steal their knowledge; however, God has released his angels to protect their knowledge. I went on further to share that angels are not these nice quiet winged creatures that we see in the movies but a commando force, heavily armed and surrounding us ready for battle.

I told these young children that an earthly example is how the secret service protects and guards the President of the United States. One child got the message so clearly she explained to her mother that if any demon came near during the exam, she believed she would hear *click! click!* as her heavily armed angels went to battle for her.

God is releasing a fresh understanding of authority and who is "the Church."

Jesus is an excellent project manager, and his project, which is you, will finish on time. Let us become the origin point of declaration against the powers of darkness.

Prayer

Father, I acknowledge your son Jesus as the excellent project manager and I am his product that will be finished in his glory and on time. I decree today that the powers of darkness are bound in Jesus' names, and what I have declared as unlawful and improper shall be not be established in my life. Amen.

Notes

Notes

Section 11

Magnetism and Electricity

Magnetism plays an important role in the study of electrical engineering. One of the fundamental laws of magnetism is that unlike poles attract and like poles repel. Many people have justified bad choices in their marriages by transferring this principle to life. Can a principle that appears in nature as in magnetism be translated into life?

When the magnetic lines which describe the magnetic field are plotted, they flow from the north pole to the south pole of the magnet. This shows a principle of completion.

There is no attraction of opposites; what we observe in magnetism is the principle of completion. The enemy has allowed this myth that opposites attract to be perpetuated, while the Bible is clear about unequal yoking.

God will allow you to be attracted to whatever and whoever is required to bring completion to your life. Yet the enemy will always bring a Delilah to you, and say that is your opposite to bring completion in your life.

For every Samson there is a Delilah, and she is not the one to bring completion in your life.

> *"You will become pregnant and have a son whose head is never to be touched by a razor because the boy is to be a Nazirite, dedicated to God from the womb. He will take the lead in delivering Israel from the hands of the Philistines." (Judges 13:5)*

God's will for Samson was that he would take the lead in delivering Israel from the hand of the Philistines. He was dedicated from the womb to be a Nazirite.

Samson began his exploits, and in Judges 14 we see that he killed a lion, then defeated and killed thirty men. In Judges 15 we see that he proceeded to kill one thousand Philistines in a battle with the jawbone of a donkey. Samson then judged Israel for twenty years with great exploits.

For every Samson there is a Delilah that claims the ability to bring completion in your life.

The word *Delilah* is from the root word *dal*, meaning "to bring low, to dry up, or to make poor."

Delilah is a spirit that is sent to dry up, and to make poor, and to make low.

Delilah was from the valley of Sorek. The name *Sorek* means "vine." The valley was a place where the best grape vines were found. It was certainly not the place for a Nazirite to be.

The Nazirites vowed not touch the grapes, raisins, grape juice, or grape wine. However it was in Sorek, the valley of grapes, that Samson fell in love with Delilah. Her strategy was to pester him daily, to press him hard and just wear him down, eventually lulling him to sleep.

The strategy of the spirit of Delilah is to pester you and to eventually wear you down until you drop you guard. This Delilah spirit has set out to bring you low, to dry you up, and to make you poor. This Delilah spirit will wear you down and grieve you to the point of death.

The Delilah spirit will attach itself to your:

- Health
- Marriage
- Children's relationships
- Finances
- Spiritual life

Samson is, however, recorded in the book of Hebrews as a hero of the faith, as the Lord remembered him and strengthened him. He pushed against the pillars and killed more Philistines when he died than when he lived.

Opposites do not attract; God will send people into your life to bring completion. As the magnetic lines of a magnet flow from its north pole to the south pole, may God also cause you to be attracted to those who will bring completion in your life.

Prayer

*Father, I ask that only the people and the things that will bring
completion in my life will flow in my direction. I cancel the
plans and schemes of Satan to send the spirit of Delilah to bring
me down low, to make me poor, and to dry me up. Let me arise
as a hero of faith in your word. Thank you, Lord. Amen.*

Notes

Notes

Section 12

Surveying

Surveying is an important aspect of the construction sector and can be defined as the art of making measurements of the relative positions of natural and man-made features on the earth's surface. This information can be presented either graphically or numerically. Surveying activities will involve measuring distances, angles, and elevations.

The Greek word for measure is *metron,* from which the English word *"meter"* comes from. So when we see the word measure in the Bible, we think of units of measurement.

There are some important kingdom principles that we need to understand concerning measure.

> *For He whom God has sent speaks the words of God, for God*
> *does not give the Spirit by measure. The Father loves the Son, and*
> *has given all things into His hand. He who believes in the Son*
> *has everlasting life; and he who does not believe the Son shall not*
> *see life, but the wrath of God abides on him.(John 3:34–36)*

God does not give the Spirit by measure. God does not give three meters of his Holy Spirit to you and six meters of his Holy Spirit to me. He gives the Holy Spirit without measure.

So we require a change in mindset. We have embraced a theology which suggests that God is a God of measure. We believe we get a cupful of the Holy Spirit at salvation and then ten years later after serving God we may get another gallon, and later a drum! So wrong.

God does not give the Spirit by measure.

We have not embraced the truth that there is a God of fullness available to us. The apostle Paul prayed for the church in Ephesus to "be filled with all the fullness of God."

For this reason I bow my knees to the Father of our Lord Jesus Christ, from whom the whole family in heaven and earth is named, that He would grant you, according to the riches of His glory, to be strengthened with might through His Spirit in the inner man, that Christ may dwell in your hearts through faith; that you, being rooted and grounded in love, 18 may be able to comprehend with all the saints what *is* the width and length and depth and height—to know the love of Christ which passes knowledge; that you may be filled with all the fullness of God. (Ephesians 3:14–19)

As a result of this mindset, we have shut God out of many aspects of our lives, and thus we have not experienced the fullness of God.

If we are truly honest with ourselves, we somehow think there are situations or circumstances in our lives in which God should not be involved. If every wife sought God in determining what to cook, their husbands would never complain about the food!

There is a place of fullness of God, where you are in constant communion with God on decision making. I make it a practice to ask God for directions when I am driving. I am not saying that I will park by the side of the road for hours waiting on God to answer which direction to go; I am saying that God speaks clearly and instantaneously.

> *Be anxious for nothing, but in everything by prayer and supplication,*
> *with thanksgiving, let your requests be made known to God; and*
> *the peace of God, which surpasses all understanding, will guard*
> *your hearts and minds through Christ Jesus. (Philippians 4:6–7)*

The words are "in everything," not in the things that cause us headaches. God is calling us to this place where we know his Spirit, which has been released from heaven to guide us into all truth, and *the Spirit has been given without measure!*

The dealings of God with Moses speak to God's interest in everything in our lives. When we look at the book of Leviticus, we see God giving directions on worship, on the environment, on health, on governance, and who you should get married to.

If God is the same God yesterday, today, and forever, a God that is unchangeable, then he is still interested in the same things in our lives. He has not changed.

God does not give his Spirit with measure, and thus we have to remove the limits on where God wishes to intervene in our lives. God wants to affect every part of your life. This is the relationship he desires, this is the fullness, and this is being complete in him.

This is the relationship God desired when Adam and Eve were in the garden of Eden. It is my desire that we all become deeply aware that God is real, and this realization causes us to be so aware of his presence that we want to do no wrong.

Prayer

Father, I thank you that you want to be involved in every aspect of my life. I desire your Holy Spirit to come into my life without measure. I need the fullness of the Holy Spirit to be evident in my life today. Amen.

Notes

Notes

Section 13

Concrete Technology

Many structures built in the Caribbean in the early 1970s are now showing signs of significant failure. In those days, it was common to mine sea sand for concrete production. After some time the salt in the sand caused the steel reinforcement to corrode, and the extreme pressure caused by the expansion of the steel during corrosion cracked the concrete. The structural member eventually failed. So every civil engineer knows that salt is detrimental to reinforced concrete.

> *You are the salt of the earth; but if the salt loses its flavor,*
> *how shall it be seasoned? It is then good for nothing but to*
> *be thrown out and trampled underfoot by men. You are the*
> *light of the world. A city that is set on a hill cannot be hidden.*
> *Nor do they light a lamp and put it under a basket, but on a*

*lampstand, and it gives light to all who are in the house. Let
your light so shine before men, that they may see your good works
and glorify your Father in heaven. (Matthew 5:13–16)*

Jesus is having his first major training session with his disciples and brings extreme correction to their theology and present way of life. He talks about this new race of people, a people released with a mandate to season the earth. He speaks of a people who are the light of the world, a people who are to give light to all and whose light should shine before men that they may see their good works and glorify God.

Salt and *light* were to be the two significant aspects of the new race. If we look in the natural world, we will glean the spiritual significance. Salt has been used to preserve meat. It is the salt that keeps the meat from deteriorating and causing a foul odor.

The salt works by extracting the water from the meat, thus denying the bacteria an important material for their growth. The saline environment is also not conducive for bacterial growth. Note these two words: *extraction* and *environment*.

Your presence ought to extract things that cause death and destruction and create an environment where sin, confusion, and destruction cannot occur. You are the salt in your home, salt in the workplace, salt in your community. You must influence what happens in the environment where you are. If you cannot influence what is happening around you, then you are useless and should thus be thrown away.

The role of the leadership in any fellowship is to point people towards saltiness. We must become a people of influence; we must be the salt of the earth.

Salt also gives food a good taste. The religion also has to be salty— indeed Christianity was meant to have good taste. But something drastically went wrong, because men have lost their salt. When you become the salt of the earth, you cause things to taste good.

The body of Christ has been trodden under the feet of men because they have lost their saltiness. Many regard the church as outdated and irrelevant, with no influence to effect change in the current affairs of the nations. When you are not salty, people walk all over you. You are trodden under the feet of men.

> *And every offering of your grain offering you shall season*
> *with salt; you shall not allow the salt of the covenant of*
> *your God to be lacking from your grain offering. With all*
> *your offerings you shall offer salt. (Leviticus 2:13)*

Every day in Old Testament times there was a grain offering on the altar, and this grain offering had to be salted. So also God wants us as the living sacrifice to be also salted each day. The other word that is relevant to us is *light*.

Physicists have defined light as the name given for a range of electromagnetic radiation that can be detected by the human eye. They believe that this radiation has a dual nature: a particle and as a wave. The amplitude of the wave is what determines the brightness of the light, and the wavelength determines the color. Quantum theory speaks of particles called photons, which are viewed by Physicists as packets of energy moving at the speed of light. According to this theory, the brightness is determined by the number of photons and the color by the energy contained in each photon.

What is your color and what is your brightness? How many packets of the energy of God are packed in you? We must understand what happens when light hits darkness; the packets of energy are moving at the speed of light and bombarding darkness. We are the ones who will destroy darkness by allowing the packets of energy that God has given us to travel at the speed of light to bombard the darkness. Such destructive light cannot be placed under a bushel.

John A. Peters

Prayer

Father, your desire is for us to be the salt of the earth and the light of the world, the salt that extracts the things that cause death and destruction, and to create an environment of love, joy, peace, kindness, and mercy. Lord, you desire us to be bright lights, showing forth to this world the brightness of your glory and destroying darkness and uprooting strongholds. Amen.

Notes

Notes

Section 14

Water Reticulation Systems

One of the principal activities involved in the treatment of water is the process called filtration. Filtration has a long history as a method of water purification, beginning in ancient Egypt. Filtration evolved from the simple Hippocratic sleeve of ancient Greece, made from cloth, to the more complicated systems as Reverse Osmosis currently on the market. Water filtration is now the premier method of water purification, removing more water contaminants, more efficiently, than any other technique.

In any filtration process there is a residue which can be simply called the *dregs*. This is waste materials that have to be disposed of. The word *dregs* is an important word in the life of a believer.

When we hear of the book of Malachi, many of us think of one verse and one topic: tithing. However, to get a full understanding of Malachi 3, we need to start to look at Malachi 1.

In the first five verses of Malachi 1, God is telling Israel through the prophet that he loves and cares for his people, and yet they say God does not love them. God then says something profound in verse 6 onwards:

A son honors *his* father,

And a servant *his* master.

If then I am the Father,

Where *is* My honor?

And if I *am* a Master,

Where *is* My reverence?

Says the Lord of hosts

To you priests who despise My name.

Yet you say, 'In what way have we despised Your name?'

"You offer defiled food on My altar,

But say,

'In what way have we defiled You?'

By saying,

'The table of the Lord is contemptible.'

And when you offer the blind as a sacrifice,

Is it not evil?

And when you offer the lame and sick,

Is it not evil?

Offer it then to your governor!

Would he be pleased with you?

Would he accept you favorably?

Says the Lord of hosts. (Malachi 1:6–8)

A son honors his father and a servant his master!

Every time we say "Father God" or "Lord God," we are making a statement to God that we will honor him. So God is saying to us today, "If then I am your father, where is my honor, and if I am your master where is my reverence?"

In verses 7 and 8, God says to the priests, "You are offering blind animals, lame and sick animals on the altar." They were bringing the dregs to God. They took the sick, lame, and blind lambs and gave this as their offering. They gave God the residue, the dregs. They filtered the best and left the rest for God.

God then poses a challenge: "Go and offer these dregs to your governor and see if he will be pleased with you and in his pleasure release favor towards you." This is a powerful truth that we need to embrace.

God will not release his favor to anyone who dishonors him, shows him no reverence, and despises his name. God is not moved by tears; he is moved by reverence and honor.

So a people that offers dregs will not receive the favor of God.

For from the rising of the sun, even to its going down,

My name *shall be* great among the Gentiles;

In every place incense *shall be* offered to My name,

And a pure offering;

For My name shall be great among the nations,"

Says the Lord of hosts.

"But you profane it,

In that you say,

'The table of the Lord is defiled;

And its fruit, its food, *is* contemptible.'

You also say,

'Oh, what a weariness!'

And you sneer at it,"

Says the Lord of hosts.

"And you bring the stolen, the lame, and the sick;

Thus you bring an offering!

Should I accept this from your hand?"

Says the Lord.

"But cursed *be* the deceiver

Who has in his flock a male,

And takes a vow,

But sacrifices to the Lord what is blemished—

For I *am* a great King,"

Says the Lord of hosts,

"And My name *is to be* feared among the
        nations. (Malachi 1: 11–14)

In verse 11, God declares that he wants a pure offering, yet in verse 13 he says that the people bring sick, lame, and stolen animals which pollute the altar. The deceiver takes a blemished lamb for the offering and leaves the best behind for himself.

So Malachi 1 is talking about a people who are offering the dregs to God. God wants the best, and instead these farmers look for all the sick, lame, near-dead, stolen animals to give as their offering.

Let us go down to Malachi 3: 8–10, which is probably one of the most misunderstood portions of Scripture.

"Will a man rob God?

Yet you have robbed Me!

But you say,

'In what way have we robbed You?'

In tithes and offerings.

You are cursed with a curse,

For you have robbed Me,

Even this whole nation.

Bring all the tithes into the storehouse,

That there may be food in My house,

And try Me now in this,"

Says the Lord of hosts,

"If I will not open for you the windows of heaven

And pour out for you *such* blessing

That *there will* not *be room* enough *to receive it.*

In verse 8 the word translated as "rob" is *qaba,* and it appears only here in Malachi and in Proverbs 22:23. It is translated as "spoil" in Proverbs and "rob" in Malachi. It is a verb.

The noun however is *qubbaath,* meaning "dregs." *Qaba* means "to offer dregs." Malachi 3:8 should thus be read, "Will a man offer dregs to God?"

This is more profound than the amount. The people at the time of Malachi were giving their one tenth, but it was from the lame, sick, stolen, and dying sheep and goats. They were filtering and offering God the dregs.

So the powerful truth revealed in Malachi 3 is not the amount of one tenth; the principle is about giving God the best, in honor and in reverence.

Today most of us are not farmers. We have developed a monetary system, and there are no lame, sick or dying bills. The principle these verses from Malachi establishes is that we must give God the best. Giving him reverence and honor opens the windows of heaven and the pouring out of the blessing that there is not room enough to receive. David understood this principle and in 1 Samuel 24:24, he placed himself to receive favor.

Then the king said to Araunah, "No, but I will surely buy it from you for a price; nor will I offer burnt offerings to the Lord my God with that which costs me nothing." So David bought the threshing floor and the oxen for fifty shekels of silver.

Prayer

Father, we come to you today, seeking repentance for every time we did not give you honor yet called you father, and every time we did not give you reverence yet called you master and lord. Forgive us this day. We will never offer dregs to you Lord, after we have filtered the best, but we will always give you our best. Amen.

Notes

Notes

Section 15

Electrical Engineering

While Benjamin Franklin is better known for his political exploits, he was also a scientist and inventor. In fact, he coined the word *battery* to describe an array of charged glass plates. The term is now part of our lives, with batteries in our cars, our cell phones, remote controls, and computers. We all have to interface with this invention of electrical engineering on a daily basis.

The cell battery has two poles, a positive and a negative. The battery produces electricity from a chemical reaction that takes place inside it. As these two poles are important in our lives in the natural world so they are in the spiritual world.

In the Jewish calendar there is a month called *Kislev*. The word means "security, trust, or positiveness."

The Jewish rabbis believed that there were two states of trust, an active and a passive trust. The active trust gave boldness and positivity, and the passive trust caused good sleep and good dreams. The rabbis believed that if one had complete trust in Jehovah God, then one would dream of the future positively.

Good dreams at night were reflective of good thoughts during the day. So when you put complete trust in Jehovah God, you would have good thoughts during the day. These good thoughts would give you good sleep and the good sleep would give you good dreams.

So what you think during the day will affect your sleep at night. Let your mind be positive and every negativity be under your feet and you will be fully charged as a believer. We have to put the positivity in our minds and the negativity under our feet.

Those who do this will have a surge of power within them, just like the battery.

> *Finally, brethren, whatever things are true, whatever things are noble, whatever things are just, whatever things are pure, whatever things are lovely, whatever things are of good report, if there is any virtue and if there is anything praiseworthy—meditate on these things. (Philippians 4:8)*

How many of us live this life? These are the positive things that should occupy our minds at all times. The things that are true about what God said about you, the thing that are true concerning what Jesus has done for you.

We worry for things that we cannot change, yet God is saying to his sons and daughters that he is Jehovah El Elyon, the most high God. If you need to be fully charged and energized for God, then you need to let your thoughts be true, noble, just, pure, lovely, of good report (the positive pole) and put the negativity under your feet.

Prayer

Father, today I choose to trust you and to believe your word to be true. I cancel every negativity thought and every negative word spoken over my life. My thoughts shall be true and noble and just and pure and lovely and of good report, and all negativity shall be under my feet. Father, energize me today, cause me to be the light of the world, and to shine your glory. Amen.

Notes

Notes

Section 16

Contract Law

In the practice of engineering, there is need to have a full understanding of contract law. The engineer needs to know the legal consequences of his or her decisions and actions and to thus avoid legal pitfalls. If engineers are aware of the conditions of contract governing the agreement, they can anticipate contractual conflicts and mitigate potential expensive situations. Sometimes lawyers have to be involved to untangle the legal conflict.

Believers also have an excellent lawyer who we sometimes fail to engage.

> *But the Helper, the Holy Spirit, whom the Father will send in My name, He will teach you all things, and bring to your remembrance all things that I said to you. Peace I leave with you, My peace I*

> *give to you; not as the world gives do I give to you. Let not your*
> *heart be troubled, neither let it be afraid. (John 14:26–28)*

In verse 26, the Greek word *parakletos* has been translated as "comforter" in some of the earlier translations and later as "helper" in versions like the New King James.

As a result of our use of language, we get different views of the word. The word *comforter* gives the impression of one patting you on the head and saying sweet things to you to soothe your pain. When our children got uneasy we gave them a comforter to keep quiet. Similarly we have viewed the Holy Spirit in the same way, someone to comfort us as when we were babies.

In the Caribbean, the word *helper* is used to describe a woman employed to clean the home and help with the laundry. Some view the Holy Spirit in that way.

However, the original Greek word was a legal term used to describe a defense attorney, the one who came to your aid in a legal matter.

Now if we begin to view the Holy Spirit as our defense attorney, our entire approach to Christian life changes. Those who have watched the famous trial of O.J. Simpson will note that when you are accused, you are finished if you have a lousy attorney.

In court, only the lawyer can present your case, only the lawyer can speak to the judge. In your interaction with your defense attorney, you have to tell all. It makes no sense lying to your defense attorney.

The Holy Spirit is your best defense attorney. He is keenly aware of every detail of your life. We therefore need to change our mindset of how we view the Holy Spirit. The Holy Spirit is a person, not a dove, or oil or a wind. He is a divine person sent by God as your defense attorney.

If we begin to see word *parakletos* as a legal word for defense attorney, we become a different people. We will be longing and searching to be always with our best defense attorney to speak for us in every conflict we encounter.

There is an accuser that we face twenty-four hours a day

> *Then I heard a loud voice saying in heaven, "Now salvation, and strength, and the kingdom of our God, and the power of His Christ have come, for the accuser of our brethren, who accused them before our God day and night, has been cast down." (Revelation 12:10)*

Night and day you are being accused, and you need your defense attorney to be there with you all the time. An intimacy develops between you and your defense attorney, as you have to be in constant dialogue. We should have a communion with our defense attorney, the Holy Spirit.

> *But Peter said, "Ananias, why has Satan filled your heart to lie to the Holy Spirit and keep back part of the price of the land for yourself? While it remained, was it not your own? And after it was sold, was it not in your own control? Why have you conceived this thing in your heart? You have not lied to men but to God." (Acts 5:3–4)*

When you lie to your defense attorney before a righteous judge, you will be judged. Ananias lied to his defense attorney and was found guilty. Thank God for the Holy Spirit, your best defense attorney.

Prayer

Father, I thank you for appointing my defense attorney, the Holy Spirit. Lord, when the accuser comes day and night to accuse, I know that the Holy Spirit is there with me at all times. I long to be with him, to share all the issues of my life, knowing that he will guide me at all times into the plans and purposes of God for my life. Amen.

Notes

Notes

Section 17

Geological Engineering

Geological engineering is the application of a combination of geology and engineering science to design that involves rock, soil, groundwater, and mineral resources.

Geological engineers carry out site investigations for dams, plants, roads, railways, housing projects, mines and quarries, pipelines, petroleum production, forestry operations, and a variety of other things. They work with civil engineers to design essential parts of projects. Geological engineers are also involved in environmental assessments or activities to clean up pollution. They prospect for minerals, building material resources and drinking water. They carry out hazard and risk assessments and map for landslides and earthquakes.

The study of geological engineering involves the study of the formation of rocks, and one kind is metamorphic rocks. One example of a metamorphic rock is marble, which begins as soft cream-colored limestone and becomes a hard and beautiful multicolored rock.

The Canaanites were a distinct people that the people of Israel had to face in constant battles. The Hebrew root word for Canaan is "low place, depress, humiliate." In modern terminology, it is a ghetto, slum, or other depressed area.

The most significant aspect of a ghetto or slum is that most times it is situated on the most expensive real estate in a city. If you look at the ghetto or slum areas in most cities of the world, you would observe that it is expensive real estate, some with the most spectacular view.

We still have to battle the Canaanite spirit today. This Canaanite spirit pushes you to never take the awesome and wonderful promises of God in your hands. You sit on the most expensive real estate and live the life of a pauper. This Canaanite spirit whispers in your ear that the slum is the best place to be, so you have no need to progress further. You have no desire for more of God.

In the natural world it is the same. There was an urban renewal project in a city in the 1980s. They moved the people who lived in a slum area to make room for a new office block. The project gave some of these people free land and assistance to build new homes in a new development.

Surprisingly, while you would think that someone would be excited to get out of a slum, some people rented their new home in the place they were relocated and went back to live in the slum. This is how the Canaanite spirit attacks.

Every believer has to recognize that the Canaanite spirit will attack. In its attack it will:

- Make you feel inferior and push you to believe that God will not hear your prayer
- Keep you in the slum of a depressed state

You will also notice chickens are quite often found in these slums. So many believers are like chickens, scratching for food, looking for food among the scraps. Yet God is looking for eagles to soar, believers who are prepared to mount up with wings as eagles do.

The Canaanite spirit will convince you that you are a chicken, that you cannot fly, and all that God has in store for you can never be obtained.

This Canaanite spirit affects how you look, how you dress, how you think, how you speak. Only the transformative power of God can break the power of this spirit.

> *I beseech you therefore, brethren, by the mercies of God, that you present your bodies a living sacrifice, holy, acceptable to God, which is your reasonable service. And do not be conformed to this world, but be transformed by the renewing of your mind, that you may prove what is that good and acceptable and perfect will of God. (Romans 12:1–2)*

The Greek word used for "transform" is the same word used to describe the biological process called metamorphosis. An example of metamorphosis is the change that takes place, such as a caterpillar changing into a butterfly.

If we see transformation as metamorphosis then we will get a clear picture as to what God has planned for us.

Look at a caterpillar. It can crawl and cannot fly. Most people do not consider it to be pleasing to the eye. It eats leaves to survive. The butterfly however cannot crawl, but can fly and is certainly a beautiful creature.

It is said that when the caterpillar is changing, all the cells die and become a liquid, and the new creature is formed from that liquid. The old creature dies for the new creature to emerge.

The geological engineer also has to understand metamorphism as a phenomenon that occurs in rock formation. The limestone is a soft cream-colored rock. However when "morphed," it becomes a hard colorful marble.

God wants that kind of transformation or metamorphism to take place in our lives. We are new creatures, no longer oppressed by the Canaanite spirit, but set free to show forth the glory of God on the earth

Prayer

Father, I thank you for sending your son Jesus to die for me, thus allowing me to be a partaker of his transformative power. I am a new creature, morphed into a person with new identity, new thinking, and new destiny. I am no longer oppressed by that Canaanite spirit, but set free to demonstrate God's glory on the earth. Amen.

Notes

John A. Peters

Notes

Section 18

Fluid Mechanics

Archimedes, that great Greek scientist and mathematician can be described as the father of fluid mechanics. One of the scientific principles he developed is known as Archimedes principle. The principle states that a body immersed in a fluid is buoyed up by a force equal to the weight of the displaced fluid. This principle applies to both floating and submerged bodies and to all fluids, i.e. liquids and gases. It explains why ships and other vessels do not sink in water but why a piece of iron will sink.

The prophet Elisha had to face Archimedes principle. Second Kings 6:1–7 has an interesting account of a miracle during the ministry of Elisha.

And the sons of the prophets said to Elisha, "See now, the place where we dwell with you is too small for us. Please, let us go to the Jordan, and let every man take a beam from there, and let us make there a place where we may dwell."

So he answered, "Go."

Then one said, "Please consent to go with your servants."

And he answered, "I will go." So he went with them. And when they came to the Jordan, they cut down trees. But as one was cutting down a tree, the iron axe head fell into the water; and he cried out and said, "Alas, master! For it was borrowed."

So the man of God said, "Where did it fall?" And he showed him the place. So he cut off a stick, and threw it in there; and he made the iron float. Therefore he said, "Pick it up for yourself." So he reached out his hand and took it.

This miracle is important to us as it speaks a profound truth that is relevant to us at this time. The sons of the prophets told Elisha that the building where the company of prophets lived, prayed, and were taught was too small. They decided to expand the building where they lived and worshipped God.

A decision was made by the prophets to go the Jordan River to get the lumber for the construction of the building. The axe of one of the young men fell into the river as he was cutting down one of the trees.

He had borrowed the axe, and he expressed concern that he would not be able to give it back. The prophet Elisha saw his distress and asked him where it fell.

Elisha took a stick, threw it in the water, and the iron axe head defied the Archimedes principle and floated to the surface. Then Elisha told the young man to pick up the axe for himself, so the young man reached out his hand and took it.

We have all been given the tools to build the Kingdom of God. The young man was given an axe to cut down trees to build a house of worship. God has given you an axe also to build his kingdom, and he expects that we sharpen the axe to accomplish that which is his purpose.

When you are cutting down trees, the constant use will dull the axe and you have to sharpen it. If you hit the tree with a dull axe, the rebound can break the axe and cause the axe head to fall off.

We have seen the effects of a dull axe in our lives. We sharpen our axe by reading the Word of God and being in continuous communion with him. You are a new creature, and the new creature has to be fed to grow. However when you starve the 'new man', you will have a dull axe, and that axe head will eventually break off.

If you want to build God's kingdom, you have to sharpen your axe, so take that file and sharpen it using the word of God and prayer.

Sadly, many have not sharpened their axes, and have lost them. But God sent a prophet. By God's grace, there will be a prophet to help you get back your axe.

It is a sad sight to see someone who has lost this axe. That person is like salt that has lost its savor: worthless. When the axe fell into the river, the young man was of no use to the building project. When you lose your axe you no longer can build God's kingdom.

God sends a prophet to ask you where your axe fell. Acknowledge that your axe head has come off and don't go trying to cut down trees with the handle; you will end up damaging your hand. We all have to come to a place where we acknowledge that our axe head has come off. There are issues in our lives that we must face and be sincere with God and say our axe head has come off.

When Elisha threw the stick into the water, the iron axe head floated to the surface. The iron sank because it was denser than the water. According to the Archimedes principle, this axe head experienced an upward force which wanted to push it out of the water, but the force of gravity pushing it down was greater.

I believe what changed was the force keeping down the axe head. Something happened when the prophet dropped that stick that caused the thing pulling the axe head down to the bottom of the river to suddenly release it.

Whatever is keeping your axe head from floating is today being removed; that thing preventing you from rising in glory to build God's kingdom is no more. Your axe head shall rise today in glory.

Elisha said to the young man to "pick it up for yourself," and he reached out his hand and took it. Today, God wants you to pick it up for yourself. No pastor can do it for you; no husband can do it for you. You have to pick up the axe head for yourself.

So reach out today, stretch out your hand, and take your miracle.

Prayer

Father, you are the same God of yesterday, today, and forever.
You are not a respecter of persons and thus if you did it for that
young man in the days of Elisha, you will do it for me today.
I acknowledge that my axe head has fallen off and I cannot
build your kingdom. Lord, remove every hindrance that is
keeping my axe head from rising to the surface. Amen.

Notes

Notes

Section 19

Global Positioning System

The Global Positioning System (GPS) is a satellite-based navigation system made up of a network of twenty-four satellites that were placed into orbit by the US Department of Defense. The system was originally intended for military use but was made available for civilian use in the 1980s.

These satellites circle the earth twice a day in a very precise orbit and transmit signal information back to earth. The GPS receivers take this information and use it to calculate the user's exact location. The GPS receiver compares the time a signal was transmitted by a satellite with the time it was received. The difference in time tells the GPS receiver the distance away the satellite is from the receiver.

If the GPS receiver is locked on to the signal of at least three satellites, then one can calculate a 2D position. When four or more satellites are in view, the receiver can determine the user's 3D position.

Your position in life depends on where you have plotted your axes. The GPS 3D position plots your latitude, longitude, and altitude. In 3D we call these the X axis, the Y axis, and the Z axis, respectively. The X and Y axis relate to your life on the earth and the Z axis deals with your relationship with God. More specifically, the X axis deals with how you relate with your family, the Y axis how you relate with your fellow man, and the Z axis with how you relate to God.

Jesus speaking to his disciples spoke this powerful truth in Matthew 22:36–40:

> *Teacher, which is the great commandment in the law?*
>
> *Jesus said to him, "'You shall love the Lord your God with all your heart, with all your soul, and with all your mind.' This is the first and great commandment. And the second is like it: 'You shall love your neighbour as yourself.' On these two commandments hang all the Law and the Prophets."*

The first and great commandment is to love the Lord with all your heart, with all your soul, and with all your mind. This is the Z axis that you have to plot.

Jesus says something very profound in verse 39. He says that the second commandment is like the first. It is also first and great!

Jesus is saying that with God there is no distinction between your love for the Lord and the love you have to show for your brother and sister. Jesus is declaring that there is no greater commandment, there is no first and second, but that they are both a total package. There can be no decoupling.

How revolutionary is this statement! Your love for God is considered as important to God as your love for your brother and sister. We have no difficulty in accepting our commitment to love our God that we cannot see, and yet we have difficulty, indeed great difficulty, in loving those we can see.

It is amazing to examine the reasons we dislike people. We either don't like their noses, we find that they talk too much, or we don't like how they speak. In fact, there are some people who we dislike from the very first time we meet them, for absolutely no reason.

> *If someone says, "I love God," and hates his brother, he is*
> *a liar; for he who does not love his brother whom he has*
> *seen, how can he love God whom he has not seen? And*
> *this commandment we have from Him: that he who loves*
> *God must love his brother also. (1 John 4: 20–21)*

Verse 21 says *must*. There is no decoupling or separation; it is one commandment.

You cannot desire to plot your Z axis as your relationship with God and fail to plot your Y axis as your relationship with your fellow man. This is what James was referring to as faith with works. Don't play holy when you are in a position to help your fellow man.

You cannot plot your Z axis as your relationship with God and fail to plot your X axis, which is your relationship with your wife, your husband, your children, and your brothers and sisters in Christ.

Many are therefore sitting on an axis and out of position with God. The word of God is the satellite that we must use to plot our position.

Are you in the right position where you are now?

John A. Peters

Prayer

Father, I desire to be in the right position in accordance with your Word. I acknowledge today that I may not be where you want me to be, and that I am not well positioned on an axis. Lord, I surrender my life to you; take me to that position which will bring glory to your name. Amen.

Notes

Notes

Section 20

Conclusion

If you have reached this point, then you will have completed the requirements to receive your degree in Christian Engineering. I believe you are now positioned to build the lives of others as you have built your own spirit through the truths released in this book.

I therefore release this prophetic word to every reader:

I pray that God will cause the eyes of your understanding to be open to receive fresh truth revealed from his heavenly throne. May you have an experience with the revealer of truth—The Holy Spirit. May he become your defense attorney against every accuser. May you learn to use the modern warfare against the enemy, and begin to launch the missiles in your arsenal to destroy every principality and power. My prayer is that your axe head will arise as every hindrance is removed today in Jesus' name.

I declare that no Canaanite spirit shall hinder you, but that you will rise in glory and be released into your destiny. May you always offer God the best and never give him the dregs. I declare that you are the salt of the earth, and God has given you a mandate to extract the things that cause death and destruction in your homes, your communities, and in your workplaces. As salt you will create an environment of love, joy, peace, kindness, and mercy.

I pray that no spirit of Delilah will bring you down low or make you poor or dry you up, but you shall arise as a hero of faith on the earth.

The Lord bless you and keep you.

The Lord make His face shine upon you this day.

The Lord be gracious to you

The Lord lift up His countenance upon you this day.

The Lord give you peace.

The Lord put his Name upon you today

Amen.